W9-BMO-659

World of Farming

Plants on a Farm

Nancy Dickmann

Heinemann Library
Chicago, Illinois

www.heinemannraintree.com
Visit our website to find out more information about Heinemann-Raintree books.

To order:
Phone 888-454-2279
Visit www.heinemannraintree.com to browse our catalog and order online.

Edited by Siân Smith, Nancy Dickmann, and Rebecca Rissman
Designed by Joanna Hinton-Malivoire
Picture research by Mica Brancic
Production by Victoria Fitzgerald
Originated by Capstone Global Library Ltd
Printed and bound in China by Leo Paper Products Ltd

ISBN 978 1 4329 3938 0
15 14 13 12
10 9 8 7 6 5 4 3 2

Library of Congress Cataloging-in-Publication Data
Dickmann, Nancy.
Plants on a farm / Nancy Dickmann.—1st ed.
p. cm.—(World of farming)
Includes bibliographical references and index.
ISBN 978-1-4329-3938-0 (hc)—ISBN 978-1-4329-3950-2 (pb)
1. Plants—Juvenile literature. 2. Farms—Juvenile literature. I. Title.
II. Series: Dickmann, Nancy. World of farming.
QK49.D52 2010
630—dc22 2009051587

Acknowledgements
We would like to thank the following for permission to reproduce photographs: FLPA p.**4** (Wayne Hutchinson); Photolibrary pp.**5** (Superstock/ Penny Adams), **6** (All Canada Photos/Peter Carroll), **7 main** (Joan Pollock), **8** (imagebroker.net/Florian Kopp), **9** (age fotostock/Javier Marina), **10** (F1 Online/Photo Thomas Gruener), **11** (fStop/Ragnar Schmuck), **12** (Garden Picture Library/Claire Higgins), **13** (Index Stock Imagery/Inga Spence), **14** (Cusp/Stock Photos/Bruce Peebles),**16** (imagebroker.net/Martin Moxter), **18** (Chad Ehlers), **19** (Tips Italia/Massimo Fornaciari), **20** (Index Stock Imagery/Lynn Stone), **21** (Blend Images/Karin Dreyer), **22** (Tips Italia/Massimo Fornaciari), **23 top** (Index Stock Imagery/Lynn Stone); Shutterstock pp.**23 bottom** (© Shvaygert Ekaterina), **7 inset** (Nikolai Pozdeev), **15** (siamionau pavel), **17** (© Shvaygert Ekaterina).

Front cover photograph of a wheat field reproduced with permission of iStockPhoto (© Devon Stephens). Back cover photograph of a girl with a pile of T-shirts reproduced with permission of Shutterstock (siamionau pavel).

The publisher would like to thank Dee Reid, Diana Bentley, and Nancy Harris for their invaluable help with this book.

Contents

What Is a Farm?

A farm is a place where food is grown.

Plants that grow on a farm are called crops.

Plants for Food

Wheat grows on a farm.

Rice grows on a farm.

Some farms grow vegetables.

Cabbages grow on a farm.

Potatoes grow on a farm.

Carrots grow on a farm.

Some farms grow fruit.

Apples grow on a farm.

Plants for Clothes and Fuel

Cotton grows on a farm.

Cotton is used to make clothes.

Corn grows on a farm.

Some corn is used to make fuel for cars.

Planting Crops

Most crops are planted in the spring.

The plants need water and sunshine to grow.

Picking Crops

Crops are usually picked in the fall.

We can buy the food grown on a farm.

Can You Remember?

What do plants need to grow?

Answer on page 24

Picture Glossary

crop plants grown on farms are called crops. Many crops are used for food.

fuel something we put into cars and trucks to make them go

Index

Answer to quiz on page 22: Plants need water and sunshine to grow.

Note to Parents and Teachers

Before reading:

Ask children if they have ever visited a farm. Ask them which plants they think grow on farms. Make a list together. What are these plants used for? Are they only for people to eat?

After reading:

- Read aloud the story of *The Little Red Hen*. Talk about what the hen has to do to grow the wheat. Ask children to imagine they are a character in the story. Then ask what that character thinks and feels at different points in the story.
- Show the children some cotton balls. Do they know where cotton grows? Show them on a map. What can they think of that is made from cotton? Ask them what other materials are used to make clothes. Do any of these materials start on a farm, too? Bring in some clothes made of cotton, wool, and linen for children to feel.